TROMBONE SHORTY

WORDS BY
**TROY
"TROMBONE SHORTY"
ANDREWS**

PICTURES BY
BRYAN COLLIER

**ABRAMS BOOKS
FOR YOUNG READERS
NEW YORK**

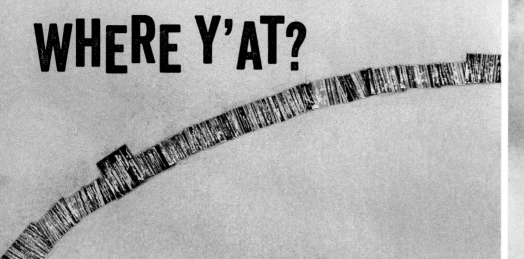

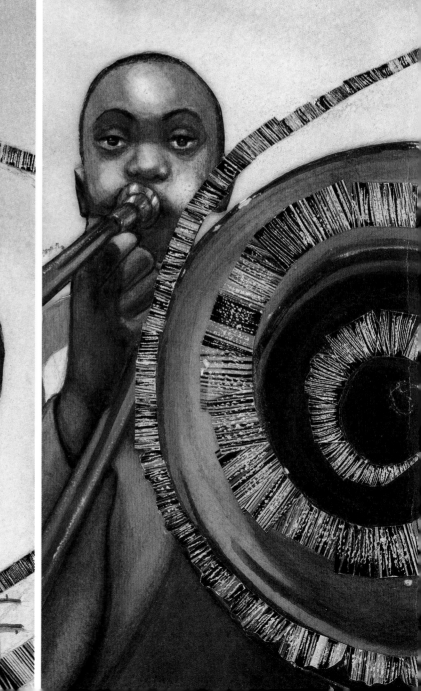

We have our own way of living down here in New Orleans, and our own way of talking, too. And that's what we like to say when we want to tell a friend hello.

So, **WHERE Y'AT?**

Lots of kids have nicknames, but I want to tell you the story of how I got mine. Just like when you listen to your favorite song, let's start at the beginning. Because this is a story about music.

But before you can understand how much music means to me, you have to know how important it is to my hometown, my greatest inspiration.

I grew up in a neighborhood in New Orleans called Tremé. Any time of day or night, you could hear music floating in the air.

And there was music in my house, too. My big brother, James, played the trumpet so loud you could hear him halfway across town! He was the leader of his own band, and my friends and I would pretend to be in the band, too.

"FOLLOW ME,"

James would say.

There's one time every year that's more exciting than any other: Mardi Gras! Parades fill the streets, and beaded necklaces are thrown through the air to the crowd.

I loved the brass bands, with their own trumpets, trombones, saxophones, and the biggest brass instrument of them all, the tuba—which rested over the musician's head like an elephant's trunk!

All day long I could see brass bands parade by
my house while my neighbors danced along. I loved
these parades during Mardi Gras because they made

everyone forget about their troubles for a little
while. People didn't have a lot of money in Tremé,
but we always had a lot of music.

I listened to all these sounds and mixed them together, just like how we make our food. We take one big pot and throw in sausage, crab, shrimp, chicken, vegetables, rice—whatever's in the kitchen—and stir it all together and let it cook. When it's done, it's the most delicious taste you've ever tried. We call it gumbo, and that's what I wanted my music to sound like—different styles combined to create my own *musical* gumbo!

But first I needed an instrument. The great thing about music is that you don't even need a real instrument to play. So my friends and I decided to make our own.

We might have sounded different from the *real* brass bands, but we felt like the greatest musicians of Tremé. We were making music, and that's all that mattered.

Then one day I found a broken trombone that looked too beaten up to make music anymore. It didn't sound perfect, but finally with a real instrument in my hand, I was ready to play.

The next time the parade went by my house, I grabbed that trombone and headed out into the street. My brother James noticed me playing along and smiled proudly.

"TROMBONE SHORTY!"

he called out, because the instrument was twice my size!

WHeRe Y'AT?

From that day on, everyone called me Trombone Shorty! I took that trombone everywhere I went and never stopped playing. I was so small that sometimes I fell right over to the ground because it was so heavy. But I always got back up, and I learned to hold it up high.

I listened to my brother play songs over and over, and I taught myself those songs, too. I practiced day and night, and sometimes I fell asleep with my trombone in my hands.

One day my mom surprised me with tickets to the New Orleans Jazz & Heritage Festival, the best and biggest music festival in town. We went to see Bo Diddley, who my mom said was one of the most important musicians of all time. As I watched him onstage, I raised my trombone to my lips and started to play along. He stopped his band in the middle of the song and asked the crowd, "Who's that playing out there?"

Everyone started pointing, but Bo Diddley couldn't see me because I was the smallest one in the place! So my mom held me up in the air and said, "That's my son, Trombone Shorty!"

"Well, **TROMBONE SHORTY,** come on up here!" Bo Diddley said.

The crowd passed me overhead until I was standing on the stage next to Bo Diddley himself! I walked right up to the microphone and held my trombone high up in the air, ready to blow.

"What do you want to play?" Bo Diddley asked.

"FOLLOW ME," I said.

After I played with Bo Diddley, I knew I was ready to have my own band. I got my friends together, and we called ourselves the 5 O'Clock Band, because that was the time we went out to play each day after finishing our homework.

We played all around New Orleans. I practiced and practiced, and soon my brother James asked me to join his band. When people wondered who the kid in his band was, he'd proudly say, "That's my little brother,

TROMBONE SHORTY!"
WHERE Y'AT?

And now I have my own band, called Trombone Shorty & Orleans Avenue, named after a street in Tremé. I've played all around the world, but I always come back to New Orleans. And when I'm home, I make sure to keep my eyes on the younger musicians in town and help them out, just like my brother did for me.

Today I play at the same New Orleans jazz festival where I once played with Bo Diddley. And when the performance ends, I lead a parade of musicians around, just like I used to do in the streets of Tremé with my friends.

WHERE Y'AT? WHERE Y'AT? WHERE Y'AT?

I still keep my
trombone in my hands,
and I will never let it go.

AUTHOR'S NOTE

I like to say that the city of New Orleans raised me. In Tremé, music was everywhere—from church, to the street, to my very own house. My grandfather, Jessie Hill, was a musician and my brother James was a musician, and I wanted to be just like them. There were people always coming and going from my house, but music was the thing we had in common. No matter how tough things got, listening to music always made me feel better.

When I was very young, my neighborhood friends and I would pretend that we were like the brass bands that would parade down our streets, and because we couldn't afford instruments, we really did make them out of whatever we could find. The box from a twelve-pack of soda could be fastened around the neck with Mardi Gras beads to become a drum, and pencils became drumsticks. I used to hoist an old Big Wheel bicycle over my shoulders and pretend it was a tuba. Empty bottles became horns and wind instruments. Thankfully, I got my first trombone when I was four years old, and by age six, I was leading my own band. The only reason I succeeded as a musician was because I practiced every day. Practicing was easy to do, because I loved playing music so much! I knew that if I just kept playing, good things would happen to me. I felt it in my bones.

I played around town with my friends for many years, and together we tried to soak in everything we could about the incredible musical traditions of New Orleans. I felt lucky that the previous generations of New Orleans musicians wanted to share their craft with me. It was my job to carry on this musical heritage.

I attended the New Orleans

TROY ANDREWS PARADING THROUGH TREMÉ

Center for Creative Arts (NOCCA) and started to develop my own musical style, one that paid tribute to New Orleans's own jazz, blues, and gospel but also mixed in other kinds of music that I loved, like rock and roll, funk, and hip-hop. I called it "SupaFunkRock." My music caught the eye of Lenny Kravitz, and at age nineteen, I joined the horn section of his band. This led to performing with other incredible musicians over the years, such as U2, Green Day, Eric Clapton, B.B. King, Prince, and many more.

I formed my own band, Trombone Shorty & Orleans Avenue, and together we've released three studio albums and even played at the Grammy Awards. In 2012, I had the honor of performing for President Barack Obama at the White House for a Black History Month celebration. In 2013, I was chosen to play the coveted closing set at the New Orleans Jazz & Heritage Festival—the same festival where I performed with Bo Diddley when I was a child.

As important as it is for me to carry the torch for the music of New Orleans, it's even more important for me to make sure that this tradition continues. In 2010, I launched the Trombone Shorty Foundation and Trombone Shorty Music Academy to make sure that the music and culture of New Orleans stay alive. While I've been fortunate enough to travel the world and share my music, I always return home to New Orleans. Nothing has been more inspiring to me than working with the

TROY ANDREWS AND BO DIDDLEY

children there. I wanted to write this book to try to inspire hope in kids who might be growing up under difficult circumstances but who also have a dream, just like I did. I'm living proof that as long as you work hard, you can make your dreams take flight.

ACKNOWLEDGMENTS

Troy Andrews would like to thank Bill Taylor, Mike Kappus, Mom and Dad, James Andrews, Susan and Bettye Scott, the Andrews family, the Matthews family, Martha Murphy, Matt Cornell, Dave Bartlett, Steve Price, and Bryan Collier.

Bill Taylor and the Trombone Shorty Foundation would like to thank Martha Murphy and the Murphy family; Joe Childress; Steve Price; Lindsay Adler; Dino Gankendorff; Tulane University; Beaux Jones; Andrew and Kerin Fredman; Rob and Susan Goldstein; Ray and Barbara Dalio; Nicole Robinson; David Kunian; John Bukaty; Danny Clinch; Tim Donnelly; Sydney Artz; Nancy Josephson; Big Chief Monk Boudreaux; Fayenisha Matthews; Rhonda Fabian; Jerry Baber Jay; Courtney, Ryan, Charlie, and Francie Taylor; and the team at Abrams, Tamar Brazis, Chad W. Beckerman, Jason Wells, Jen Graham, and Susan Van Metre.

ILLUSTRATOR'S NOTE

The images for *Trombone Shorty* were painted in watercolor and collage. I felt it was important to depict the sound of the music as beautiful colors and shapes that swirl out of Troy's trombone. Even the balloons that you see dancing throughout the book represent music always being around and floating through the air. By the end of the book, these balloons have transformed into a large hot-air balloon, powered by the force of Troy Andrews's horn. This balloon first transports Troy's musical message over the city of New Orleans, but as Troy grows, his music has the power to soar over the entire world.

One of my favorite images in this book is the one of Troy and his friends with their homemade instruments. The neighborhood called Faubourg Tremé, now known as Tremé, where Troy was born and raised, is both historic and musically rich. Troy always had music and musical heroes to look up to, like his big brother, James, but becoming a great musician takes a lot of practice, hard work, and sacrifice. And you need instruments. The fact that Troy and his friends constructed their own makeshift instruments until they could get real ones conveyed both their strong desire to imitate the older musicians they loved and to make music themselves. To me, this showed the hope and promise in these boys. So I decided to give them crowns in my painting, because, early on, they were like royalty.

I've been lucky enough to spend time with Troy Andrews and experience what a warmhearted person and amazing talent he is. I was blown away as I watched Troy mesmerize crowds time and time again with his horn play. I'm honored to be a part of this book, and I can't wait for our next collaboration.

Courtesy of Danny Clinch

TROY "TROMBONE SHORTY" ANDREWS

ABOUT THE TROMBONE SHORTY FOUNDATION

The mission of the Trombone Shorty Foundation is to preserve the rich musical history of New Orleans.

The Trombone Shorty Foundation and Tulane University partnered to create the Trombone Shorty Music Academy, which provides music and business education, instruction, and a mentorship experience to New Orleans high school students who are gifted in music. Experienced instructors help young, underserved musicians express themselves and pursue their dreams while also supporting their community.

Please visit www.tromboneshortyfoundation.org.

TO ALL THE MUSICIANS IN THE GREAT
CITY OF NEW ORLEANS—PAST, PRESENT,
AND FUTURE. —TA

TO EVERYONE WITH EYES TO SEE AND EARS
TO HEAR THE EXTRAORDINARY MUSICIAN
TROY ANDREWS. —BC

The illustrations in this book were made with pen
and ink, watercolor, and collage.

Library of Congress
Cataloging-in-Publication Data
Andrews, Troy, author.
Trombone Shorty / by Troy Andrews and
Bill Taylor ; illustrated by Bryan Collier.
pages cm
ISBN 978-1-4197-1465-8 (hardcover)
1. Andrews, Troy—Juvenile literature. 2. Jazz
musicians—United States—Juvenile literature.
3. Trombonists—United States—Juvenile literature. I. Taylor, Bill, 1971-, author. II. Collier, Bryan,
illustrator. III. Title.
ML3930.A53A3 2015
788.9'3165092—dc23
[B]
2014016106

Text copyright © 2015 Troy Andrews and Bill Taylor
Illustrations copyright © 2015 Bryan Collier
Book design by Chad W. Beckerman

Printed and bound in U.S.A.
10 9 8 7 6 5 4 3

Abrams Books for Young Readers are available at
special discounts when purchased in quantity for
premiums and promotions as well as fundraising or
educational use. Special editions can also be created
to specification. For details, contact specialsales@
abramsbooks.com or the address below.

ABRAMS
THE ART OF BOOKS SINCE 1949

115 West 18th Street
New York, NY 10011
www.abramsbooks.com